Biblical Foundation 9

Authority
and
Accountability

by Larry Kreider

House To House Publications
Lititz, Pennsylvania USA

Authority and Accountability

Larry Kreider

Updated Edition © 2002, Reprinted 2003, 2006
Copyright © 1993, 1997, 1999
House to House Publications
11 Toll Gate Road, Lititz, PA 17543
Telephone: 800.858.5892
Web site: www.dcfi.org

ISBN 10: 1-886973-08-3
ISBN 13: 978-1-886973-08-4
Design and illustrations by Sarah Sauder

Biblical Foundations

CONTENTS

Books in this Series

This is the ninth book in a twelve-book series designed to help believers to build a solid biblical foundation in their lives.

A corresponding *Biblical Foundations for Children* book is also available (see page 63).

Introduction

The foundation of the Christian faith is built on Jesus Christ and His Word to us, the Holy Bible. This twelve-book *Biblical Foundation Series* includes elementary principles every Christian needs to help lay a strong spiritual foundation in his or her life.

In this ninth Biblical Foundation book, *Authority and Accountability,* we learn that the Lord has chosen to give His authority to men and women in various areas including the government, our employment, the church and our families. If we have a healthy understanding of the fear of the Lord, we will understand why God places authorities in our lives. The Lord delegates responsibility to the authorities so that He can use them to bring protection, adjustment and structure into our lives. A proper understanding of authority will bring security into our lives.

In this book, the foundation truths from the Word of God are presented with modern day parables that help you easily understand the basics of Christianity. Use this book and the other 11 *Biblical Foundation* books to lay a solid spiritual foundation in your life, or if you are already a mature Christian, these books are great tools to assist you in discipling others. May His Word become life to you today.

God bless you!
Larry Kreider

How to Use This Resource

Personal study

Read from start to finish as an individual study program to build a firm Christian foundation and develop spiritual maturity.

- Each chapter has a key verse excellent to commit to memory.
- Additional scriptures in gray boxes are used for further study.
- Each reading includes questions for personal reflection and room to journal at the end of the book.

Daily devotional

Use as a devotional for a daily study of God's Word.

- Each chapter is divided into 7-day sections for weekly use.
- Additional days at the end of the book bring the total number of devotionals to one complete month. The complete set of 12 books gives one year's worth of daily devotionals.
- Additional scriptures are used for further study.
- Each day includes reflection questions and a place to write answers at the end of the book.

Mentoring relationship

Use for a spiritual parenting relationship to study, pray and discuss life applications together.

- A spiritual father or mother can easily take a spiritual son or daughter through these short Bible study lessons and use the reflection questions to provoke dialogue about what is learned.
- Read each day or an entire chapter at a time.

Small group study

Study this important biblical foundation in a small group setting.

- The teacher studies the material in the chapters and teaches, using the user-friendly outline provided at the end of the book.

Taught as a biblical foundation course

These teachings can be taught by a pastor or other Christian leader as a basic biblical foundation course.

- Students read an assigned portion of the material.
- In the class, the leader teaches the assigned material using the chapter outlines at the end of the book.

CHAPTER 1

Understanding the Fear of the Lord and Authority

KEY MEMORY VERSE
The fear of the Lord is the
beginning of wisdom...
Proverbs 1:7

The fear of the Lord causes us to obey

Jonah was a prophet in the Old Testament who made a major mistake. The Lord called him to go to the wicked city of Nineveh and warn the people of God's impending judgment. But Jonah knew that his God was a compassionate God. He figured that the people in Ninevah would repent and be spared God's judgment, and he really did not want God to have mercy on any nation but Israel. So, instead of obeying, he boarded a ship that was going in the opposite direction to the farthest place possible.

In the midst of the voyage, the Lord sent a huge storm that nearly wiped out the ship. The sailors were frightened as they cried out to their heathen gods. In the turmoil, someone found Jonah asleep in the lower part of the ship. The captain implored Jonah, "What are you doing sleeping? Get up and call on your God; maybe He'll keep us from perishing!"

Even though the sailors did not believe in the true God, they were spiritual men and believed in the supernatural. They cast lots to see whether or not someone on board was the cause of the storm that was about to destroy them. The lot fell on Jonah. Jonah then confessed...*I fear the Lord, the God of heaven, who made the sea and the dry land (Jonah 1:9 NKJ).*

Jonah felt guilty for disobeying God and putting the sailors at risk. He instructed the sailors to pick him up and throw him into the sea and promised that the sea would then stop raging. After repeated attempts to bring the ship to land, but to no avail, they reluctantly threw Jonah overboard. Immediately the sea grew calm. *At this the men greatly feared the Lord, and they offered a sacrifice to the Lord and made vows to him (Jonah 1:16).*

These men understood the fear of the Lord. The fear of the Lord causes people to place their faith in the Lord for salvation. It also causes them to realize that God judges sin because He is a holy God. We need to have a healthy understanding of the fear of the Lord. If we understand the fear of the Lord, we will want to live a life of obedience to Him.

REFLECTION
In the story of Jonah, how did the sailor's fear of their heathen gods differ from the fear of the Lord they experienced in Jonah 1:16?

Biblical Foundations

The fear of the Lord causes us to reverence God

The Bible tells us in Proverbs 9:10a that if we have a deep reverence and love for God, we will gain wisdom. *The fear of the Lord is the beginning of wisdom....*

A healthy understanding of the fear of the Lord is simply to be awestruck by His power and presence. *To fear the Lord* means *to be in awe and to reverence the Lord,* understanding that we serve a mighty God. Our Father in heaven loves us perfectly. He wants the best for our lives. He is a God who has created the entire universe and has all power and authority in His hand. As Christians, we should possess a holy fear that trembles at God's Word. *"Has not my hand made all these things, and so they came into being?" declares the Lord. "This is the one I esteem: he who is humble and contrite in spirit, and trembles at my word" (Isaiah 66:2).*

This is not to say that God wants us to cower in a corner.

REFLECTION

If God does not want us to be afraid of Him, what kind of "fear" are we talking about?

That's not what the fear of the Lord is about. The Lord does not desire for His children to be afraid of Him, but to honor and respect Him. God's Word tells us that "perfect love casts out fear" (1 John 4:18). In other words, where there is God's perfect love, fear cannot dwell; or to say it another way— where there is the presence of fear, there is the absence of love.

However, if we love, honor and respect our God, we will want to obey Him because the fear of the Lord also involves a fear of sinning against Him and facing the consequences. I grew up with an earthly father who loved me. I was not afraid of him. However, whenever I was disobedient, I feared the consequences of the discipline I knew would follow. Yet, I knew that even the discipline was from a father who loved me. Our heavenly Father loves us so much, yet He hates sin.

Our God is a God of complete authority in this universe. Ask the Lord to give you the grace to experience the fear of the Lord in your life. Expect to be awestruck by His presence in your life!

① Reverence, gratitude, respectful esteem, meekness + humility on our end.

The fear of the Lord causes us to turn away from evil

When we have a healthy fear of the Lord, we will not want to sin against Him. *To fear the Lord is to hate evil...(Proverbs 8:13).* We know that sinning against a holy God means we will have to face the consequences. Although we realize that God is not a God with a big stick just waiting for us to make a mistake, God *will* punish sin.

The Bible tells us in Acts 9:31 that the New Testament church understood what it meant to walk in the fear of the Lord. When we have a proper understanding of the fear of the Lord, we will hate evil, knowing that evil displeases the Lord and destroys God's people. *Do you not know that the wicked will not inherit the kingdom of God? Do not be deceived: Neither the sexually immoral nor idolaters nor adulterers nor male prostitutes nor homosexual offenders nor thieves nor the greedy nor drunkards nor slanderers nor swindlers will inherit the kingdom of God. And that is what some of you were. But you were washed, you were sanctified, you were justified in the name of the Lord Jesus Christ and by the Spirit of our God (1 Corinthians 6:9-11).*

In other words, true Christians will not live a life of sin. The good news is this: when we repent and turn from our sin, Jesus washes us clean. And the "fear of the Lord" keeps us from going back to our old way of living.

There are many examples of the fear of the Lord in the New Testament. After Ananias and Sapphira lied to the Holy Spirit and were struck dead, God's judgment on their sin caused the believers to increase in their awe and fear of the Lord. *Great fear seized the whole church and all who heard about these events (Acts 5:11).*

In Revelation 1:17, John had an encounter with God. *When I saw him, I fell at his feet as though dead. Then he placed his right hand on me and said: "Do not be afraid. I am the First and the Last."*

REFLECTION

What do we hate when we have a healthy fear of the Lord, according to Proverbs 8:13?
What does the fear of the Lord lead us to?

Our fear of the Lord is not a destructive fear but one that leads us to God's presence and purity. When we understand and experience the fear of the Lord, we will hate sin and turn away from it. We will trust Jesus to wash, cleanse and make us new.

† sin/evil
† repentance, presence, purity.

Why authorities are placed in our lives

The Lord has chosen to give His authority to men and women in various areas including the government, our employment, the church and our families. If we understand the fear of the Lord in a healthy way, we will understand why God places authorities in our lives. The Lord delegates responsibility to the authorities so that He can use them to mold us, adjust us, and structure our lives. If we resist these authorities, scripture indicates we are resisting God and bringing judgment upon ourselves. Romans 13:1-4a tells us, *Everyone must submit himself to the governing authorities, for there is no authority except that which God has established. The authorities that exist have been established by God. Consequently, he who rebels against the authority is rebelling against what God has instituted, and those who do so will bring judgment on themselves. For rulers hold no terror for those who do right, but for those who do wrong. Do you want to be free from fear of the one in authority? Then do what is right and he will commend you. For he is God's servant to do you good....*

The authorities that are in our lives have been placed there by God. For example, police officers and government officials are ministers of God. That does not mean they are being obedient to God all of the time. However, God has placed them in our lives and wants us to respond to them in a godly way. If we're driving through a town and a police officer stands at an intersection and puts up his hand, every driver will stop because of his authority. It is not his own authority, but the authority of the government he represents. If we disobey the police officer, we are disobeying the government, because the police officer is under authority.

A proper understanding of authority will bring security into our lives. The scriptures teach us that "rulers hold no terror for those who do right, but for those who do wrong" (Romans 13:3). When there is no authority, there is chaos. One of the darkest periods of history for the people of God occurred because no authority was set in place. *In those days Israel had no king; everyone did as he saw fit (Judges 21:25).* Society does not tolerate chaos. There is always a need for some form of government or type of authority structure. If we do not have a godly authority structure, the vacuum will cause an ungodly authority structure to develop.

Is There?

God delegates His authority to men and women. Anyone who has authority needs to be under authority, or he becomes a tyrant. I once heard a story of a sergeant in the army who relished his authority, taking great pleasure in telling men to obey his orders. When he retired, he attempted to apply the same principles in his hometown. He would bark an order at a store clerk, or a mail carrier, or a waiter in a restaurant. Needless to say, he was not very well received! The ex-sergeant soon realized he no longer had authority over those people, because he was no longer under (military) authority.

If we are not under the authority of Jesus, we can attempt to resist the devil and the demons of hell, but they do not need to submit to us. However, when we are submitted to God's authority in our lives, the devil must flee.

REFLECTION
Who are the governing authorities in your life? List ways each one is used by the Lord to mold, adjust and structure your life.

DAY 5

What does it mean to submit to authority?

The Lord has set up delegated authorities to protect us and to help mold, adjust and structure us to be conformed to the image of Christ. For many people, this is a hard lesson to learn. There was a young man who was not willing to submit to the authority of his parents so he decided to join the army. Guess what? Now, he *really* learned to understand what submitting to authority was all about!

What does it mean to "submit to authority?" The word *submit* means *to yield, stand under, defer to the opinion or authority of another.* Submission is an attitude of the heart that desires to obey God and the human authorities that He has placed in our lives.

The word *authority* means *a right to command or act.* In other words, it is *the right given by God to men and women to build, to mold, and to adjust and structure the lives of others.* An authority is a person who has been given responsibility for our lives. At our workplace, it's our employer; in our hometown, it is our local government official; in the body of Christ, our authorities are the elders and pastors of our church; and for young people who are living at home, it is their parents.

Paul reminds believers in Titus 3:1 that it is important to be obedient to the authorities in their lives. *Remind the people to be*

✱ Customers, Fred, Bob, probation officer etc...

✱ opportunity for witness, opportunity to learn
opportunity to see God's promise of blessing if
done right, opportunity to be taught + be meek

subject to rulers and authorities, to be obedient, to be ready to do whatever is good.

Submission to authority is not a popular topic today. Employees rebel against their employers, school children against their teachers, children against their parents and churchgoers against their pastors. The Lord wants to restore a proper understanding of the fear of the Lord and submission to authority to our generation. If we do not learn to properly submit to the authorities the Lord has placed in our lives, we are disobedient to God who has placed these authorities there.

REFLECTION
What does authority mean? How is resisting authority in your life actually resisting God?

right to command or act.
God placed them in authority over us

Submission to authority seems foolish to many people, *but God chose the foolish things of the world to shame the wise; God chose the weak things of the world to shame the strong (1 Corinthians 1:27).*

Whenever I resist any authority the Lord has placed in my life— parents, employer, police, church authority—I am actually resisting God. (Unless, of course, the authority is asking me to do something that violates God's Word and causes me to sin. See Chapter 2, Day 4). I have told young people, "When your parents ask you to be in by midnight or an employer tells you to be at work on time, the Lord is using these authorities to train and mold you into the character of Christ. If you don't obey, you will have to learn the same hard lessons over and over again."

Obedience is better than "sacrifice"

God always requires obedience to His Word. In 1 Samuel 15:22-23, Saul rebelled and disobeyed God's clear instructions because he placed his own perception of what was right above what God said. Saul had been commanded to wait until the prophet Samuel came to offer a sacrifice. However, Saul feared the people instead of fearing God, and went ahead and offered the sacrifice. Samuel's admonition was very direct and to the point...*does the Lord delight in burnt offerings and sacrifices as much as in obeying the voice of the Lord? To obey is better than sacrifice, and to heed is better than the fat of rams. For rebellion is like the sin of divination, and arrogance like the evil of idolatry....*

He misdirected his fear + rushed ahead of Gods commandment + did it his way.

It wasn't the sacrifice that pleased God
It was the obeying Him to the letter from your heart that pleased Him
humble.

DAY 6

Obeying from the heart is better than "sacrifice" (any outward form of service for the Lord). Rebellion (disobedience) is equated with the sin of witchcraft. Later, the Bible tells us that an evil spirit tormented Saul (1 Samuel 16:14). Saul's rebellion allowed room for an evil spirit to come into his life, and he lived as a tormented man for the rest of his life. He had refused to walk in the fear of the Lord.

Unless we learn to submit to the authorities the Lord has placed in our lives, we cannot respond appropriately as an authority to others. Children who do not obey their parents and do not repent for their disobedience grow up with an unwholesome understanding of authority. They are often domineering over their own children. If we have not properly responded to the authorities the Lord has placed in our lives, the Lord may require us to ask

REFLECTION
What did Saul do that displeased God so much? Explain the phrase "obedience is better than sacrifice."

forgiveness of the person(s) we have dishonored. Our confession can break the bondage of rebellion and stubbornness that may be operating in our lives.

Delegated authority molds us

The authorities the Lord has placed in our lives will not be perfect. We do not submit to them because they are perfect, but we submit to them because the Lord has placed them there. I remember one of the jobs I had as a young man. I did not like the attitude of my employer. But, regardless of his attitude, I submitted to him because he was my employer. I have learned that it is a tremendous blessing to obey the authorities the Lord has placed in my life.

Wherever we go, one of the first questions we should ask ourselves is, "Who has the Lord placed in authority here?" People who are truly under God's authority see authority everywhere they go. They realize these authorities have been delegated and appointed by the Lord. Luke 17:7-10 explains this delegated authority. *Suppose one of you had a servant plowing or looking after the sheep. Would he say to the servant when he comes in from the field, "Come along now and sit down to eat"? Would he not rather say, "Prepare my supper, get yourself ready and wait on me while I eat and drink; after that you may eat and drink"? Would he thank the servant because he did what he was told to do? So you also, when you have*

Biblical Foundations

done everything you were told to do, should say, "We are unworthy servants; we have only done our duty."

This slave, after working hard all day, came in from the field and prepared his master's meal first. Did his master thank him? No, because it was the *responsibility* of the servant to prepare the food for his master. The servant had a clear understanding of God's delegated authority. Secure people have no problem with submitting to the authorities the Lord has placed in their lives.

It is our responsibility to submit to the authorities the Lord has placed in our lives, in our homes, employment, community and in the church. The Lord works His character in us as we learn this important principle. I have seen it happen over and over again when someone cannot submit to his employer—in most cases, he goes from job to job with the same problem, because the problem lies with the employee. The Lord uses His delegated authorities to teach us, mold us, and build the character of Christ in our lives. We, then, can be His loving authorities to others whom He places in our lives.

REFLECTION
Put yourself in the place of the servant in this story. What would your attitude be?

* I have been there
+ it was a struggle but we
learn - for me God pushed
+ placed me in greener pastures
praise God

CHAPTER 2

Delegated Authority in Government, Workplace, Family and Church

KEY MEMORY VERSE

...for there is no authority except that which God has established...Consequently, he who rebels against the authority is rebelling against what God has instituted...

Romans 13:1-2

Honoring authority in government

In this chapter, we're going to look at four basic areas where God has delegated His authority to men and women. These four areas include the government, the workplace, the family and the church.

First of all, let's look at government. In the fallen world we live in, we need order and restraints to protect us from chaos. That's why God ordained government. According to Romans 13:1-2 we are to submit to the governing authorities. *Everyone must submit himself to the governing authorities, for there is no authority except that which God has established...Consequently, he who rebels against the authority is rebelling against what God has instituted....*

Christians should obey the governing authorities because they are instituted by God. Romans 13:5-7 says we should be subject to authorities not because we are afraid of punishment but because they have been ordained by God and we must keep a clear con-science by obeying them: *Therefore, it is necessary to submit to the authorities, not only because of possible punishment but also because of conscience. This is also why you pay taxes, for the authorities are God's servants, who give their full time to governing. Give everyone what you owe him: If you owe taxes, pay taxes; if revenue, then revenue; if respect, then respect; if honor, then honor.* This scripture says that if we complain about paying taxes, we are complaining about the authorities the Lord has placed in our lives.

Obeying governmental authorities
Matthew 17:24-27; 22:15-22
Romans 13:1-7
1 Peter 2:13-17

Sometimes we tend to speak negatively about authorities—police officers, for example. We especially do this when they give us a ticket for a traffic violation! We must remember that police officers are God's ministers. We need to relate to them with a submissive attitude of honor.

REFLECTION
Why should we be careful who we call a "whitewashed wall"? Why should we honor governmental authorities?

Daniel, in the Old Testament, was taken to Babylon as a slave when he was sixteen years old. Even so, he lived in the fear of the Lord and was a man of prayer. He learned to honor the leadership in Babylon and was appointed prime minister under three different administrations.

Whether or not authorities in our lives are godly or ungodly people, the Lord has placed them there. One time, Apostle Paul was taken before the religious council. The high priest, Ananias, commanded those who stood by Paul to strike him on the mouth. Paul didn't realize Ananias was the high priest and responded by calling him a "whitewashed wall" (Acts 23:3). Those standing by said, "How can you insult God's high priest?" Paul immediately apologized...*Brothers, I did not realize that he was the high priest; for it is written: "Do not speak evil about the ruler of your people"* (Acts 23:5).

Even though the authorities in our lives may be ungodly, the Lord has called us to have an attitude of submission to them. We honor them for their position, not for their conduct.

Honoring authority in the workplace

DAY 2

The second group of authorities the Lord has placed in our lives are our employers. Paul urges Christians to regard their jobs as service to the Lord. *Slaves, [employees] obey your earthly masters [employers] in everything; and do it, not only when their eye is on you and to win their favor, but with sincerity of heart and reverence for the Lord. Whatever you do, work at it with all your heart, as working for the Lord, not for men, since you know that you will receive an inheritance from the Lord as a reward. It is the Lord Christ you are serving* (Colossians 3:22-24).

In other words, our real employer is Jesus Christ. We need to see our jobs as serving the Lord Jesus Christ. If we have a tendency to do our best only when the boss is around, then there's a problem.

I have a friend who worked in a steak restaurant. He submitted to his boss as the authority he knew the Lord had placed over him. The owners and managers were so impressed with his attitude, they continued to hire his Christian friends. Within a short period of time, the majority of the employees at the restaurant were Christians. Why? Because this young man had an attitude of submission to the authority of his managers and employers.

REFLECTION

How are we really working for "employer" Jesus Christ on our jobs? What should our attitude be toward our employers?

① He not only places masters over us but He is the rewarder of our faithfulness.

Authority and Accountability

② Regard them as we would Christ,

19

The Lord has called us to work at our jobs enthusiastically with all of our hearts, realizing we are doing it unto the Lord. And imagine, as we're doing it unto the Lord, we are getting paid to serve Him in our places of employment!

How God uses employers in our lives

If your boss is a Christian, do not think he should give you extra favors because you are a believer. Some Christians think, "My boss should understand why I'm late to work or why I'm slow. He is a Christian." Even if he is a believer, your boss needs to take the authority given to him by God and discipline you so that you can be truly conformed into the image of Christ.

All who are under the yoke of slavery [employees] should consider their masters [employers] worthy of full respect, so that God's name and our teaching may not be slandered. Those who have believing masters are not to show less respect for them because they are brothers. Instead, they are to serve them even better, because those who benefit from their service are believers, and dear to them...(1 Timothy 6:1-2).

Slaves [employees], submit yourselves to your masters [employers] with all respect, not only to those who are good and considerate, but also to those who are harsh. For it is commendable if a man bears up under the pain of unjust suffering because he is conscious of God. But how is it to your credit if you receive a beating for doing wrong and endure it? But if you suffer for doing good and you endure it, this is commendable before God. To this you were called, because Christ suffered for you, leaving you an example, that you should follow in his steps (1 Peter 2:18-21).

If we are late for work or lazy on the job, our employer needs to deal with us properly so we can learn to be disciplined men and women of God. However, if we are doing a good job and our employer is harsh or critical, then the Lord promises us that He will reward us.

REFLECTION

How should we act if we are disciplined on the job by a believing boss for doing something wrong?

How is Jesus our example in the matter of submission?

① respectful & with humility

② He submitted even to earthly authorities (His own creation) because He knew His Father has

Biblical Foundations

put them in place.

Jesus and Moses both learned to submit to their employer's authority before the Lord used them effectively. Jesus worked in the carpenter's shop for many years before being thrust into His ministry (Mark 6:3). Moses was herding sheep for his father-in-law for 40 years as God prepared him for leadership to lead the Lord's people out of the bondage of Egypt (Exodus 3). Their heavenly Father used these authorities in their lives to teach them to have a submissive spirit toward Him and a spirit of patience toward the people whom they served.

Honoring authority in the family

The Lord has instructed us to submit to the authorities that He has placed in our lives. Families are another area of submission. Ephesians 6:1-4 tells us, *Children, obey your parents in the Lord, for this is right. "Honor your father and mother"—which is the first commandment with a promise—"that it may go well with you and that you may enjoy long life on the earth." Fathers, do not exasperate your children; instead, bring them up in the training and instruction of the Lord.*

God commands children to obey the authorities He's placed in their lives, namely their parents. To the obedient, He promises a long life! Children who honor their parents will be blessed by God here on earth.

Parents, too, must honor their children. They honor them by submitting to the needs of their children—bringing them up in the instruction of the Lord without discouraging them with unrealistic expectations (Colossians 3:21).

Many times young people have asked me if they should obey their parents when their parents are not Christians and ask them to do something that is not right in God's sight. Acts 5:29b tells us that... *we must obey God rather than men!*

If any authority in our lives asks us to do something that is sin, we need to obey God first! For example, Kako was a young Christian believer whose Buddhist parents wanted her to continue to at-

REFLECTION
*What is the promise for those who honor their parents (Ephesians 6:1-4)?
According to Acts 5:29, what should we do if an authority in our lives asks us to do something that is sinful?*

① All will go well + long life

② Obey God 1st + refuse sin.

tend and participate in their religious rituals. She could not obey her parents by continuing to worship these false gods and refused. God was her higher authority. Our obedience to any authority must always be based on a higher loyalty to God. So then, if parents or any other authority in our lives asks us to do anything that is against the Word of God, we need to obey God first. (See Chapter 3, Day 5.)

Submit to each other in the home

To be in "submission" is to be *under the authority of the one responsible for the mission of our lives.* At work, we are *under the mission* of our employer. In school, we are *under the mission* of our teacher. On a basketball team, we are *under the mission* of the coach. In the church, we are *under the mission* of the spiritual leadership the Lord has placed in our lives. And in our homes, we are *under the mission* of the head of our home. Let's see how mutual submission is a principle applied to Christian families. *Submit to one another out of reverence for Christ. Wives, submit to your husbands as to the Lord. For the husband is the head of the wife as Christ is the head of the church, his body, of which he is the Savior (Ephesians 5:21-23).*

In families, the Lord has called husbands and wives to submit to each other. God wants husbands and wives to be in unity as a team. However, in every team, there's always someone the Lord places as leadership in that team. In the case of the husband and wife, the Bible says the husband is the head of the wife. His leadership must be exercised in love and consideration for his family. A husband has the responsibility to love his wife the same way Jesus Christ loved His church and gave His life for it (Ephesians 6:25).

As the leader in the home, a husband is responsible, in times of crisis, to make final decisions. A few years ago, my wife and I needed to make a decision about whether or not to send our children to a Christian school. We prayed and talked and prayed and talked, but finally we had to make a decision. My wife's response was that as the head of the home, I needed to make the decision and she would submit to my leadership. She trusted

REFLECTION
How do husbands and wives submit to each other?
Who should take leadership for the husband-wife team?

① In love & unity.

② Whoever wants to be the one to answer
for both rewards & discipline for both righteous.
yur righteous, just & unjust leadership... standard bible answer ; husband

Biblical Foundations

the Lord to lead me in making the right decision.

In a single parent home, the Lord gives special grace to moms and dads who do not have spouses to help them raise their children. The Bible says that our God is a father to the fatherless (Psalm 68:5). The Lord also desires to use the body of Christ (the local church) to assist moms and dads who are single parents (James 1:27).

Honoring authority in the church

The fourth area of authority the Lord delegates to men and women is in the church. Hebrews 13:17 says, *Obey your leaders and submit to their authority. They keep watch over you as men who must give an account. Obey them so that their work will be a joy, not a burden, for that would be of no advantage to you.*

The Lord places spiritual authorities in our lives who watch over us and must give an account to the Lord for our spiritual lives. The Lord has placed elders and pastors in our lives to direct, correct and protect us. That's why it's so important for every believer to be connected to the local church; it brings spiritual protection to us.

Paul was willing to be accountable to the spiritual leaders the Lord had placed in his life. When Paul and Barnabas were sent out of the church of Antioch to plant churches throughout the world, they returned to their local church a few years later and reported all that the Lord had done (Acts 14:27-28).

We should honor the spiritual leaders the Lord has placed in our lives according to 1 Thessalonians 5:12-13. *Now we ask you, brothers, to respect those who work hard among you, who are over you in the Lord and who admonish you. Hold them in the highest regard in love because of their work. Live in peace with each other.*

I meet people who say, "I don't agree with my pastor or my church leadership." I first encourage them to pray for God's blessing and wisdom on their spiritual leaders. After that, the Lord may also want them to appeal to their leaders in love about those issues, keeping in mind that they cannot change their leaders—that is God's responsibility. If the differences persist, they may also need to consider two other possibilities—maybe they have rebellion in their lives they need to deal with, or perhaps the Lord has called them to another church.

Jesus, when teaching His disciples about leadership, instructed them to not be like the Gentiles who rule over others, but to be servants (Matthew 20:25-28). Jesus was not suggesting that spiritual leaders have no responsibility or authority to give direction to the church, but that their attitude should be that of a servant. Spiritual authority and servanthood go hand-in-hand. For example, Nehemiah in the Old Testament, was a man of authority, but he did not lord it over the people like former governors (Nehemiah 5:15). He was a servant who walked in the fear of the Lord.

The Lord's call on spiritual leaders is to help each believer draw closer to Jesus and learn from Him. The Lord has called us to have an attitude of submission toward the leaders He has placed in our lives. Years ago I heard a story of a little

REFLECTION
How do we honor spiritual authorities in our lives? What are the things our spiritual authorities do for us?

boy who insisted on standing on his chair during a church meeting. When his father took his hand and pulled him down into a seated position, the little boy looked up at his father and said, "I may be sitting down on the outside, but I'm standing up on the inside!" The Lord is concerned about our heart attitudes.

To summarize, we are called to pray, support, submit and appeal to our spiritual authorities. (We will talk more about appealing to authority in the next chapter). Likewise, our spiritual authorities—pastors and elders—should pray for us, teach us, protect us and correct us as we need it.

Sin in a spiritual leader's life

DAY 7

What happens if a spiritual leader falls into sin? We should not blindly submit to a leader who has sin in his life but instead confront him according to 1 Timothy 5:19-20. *Do not entertain an accusation against an elder unless it is brought by two or three witnesses. Those who sin are to be rebuked publicly, so that the others may take warning.*

If someone with spiritual authority (elder, pastor, cell leader, house church leader, etc.) sins and it is confirmed, those whom are placed over him spiritually are responsible to discipline him. Most local churches are a part of a larger "family of churches" or a denomination. The leadership of this family of churches has the responsibility, along with the other elders, to administer proper discipline. In fact, the Bible says the guilty one should be rebuked

① submit, give an account to + remain connected to spiritual leaders.

② Keep watch over us spiritually protect us, help us draw closer to God. Make + take an account for us. pray, teach protect, + correct.

in the presence of everyone in the church. This is why all leaders should also have spiritual authorities who will give them the direction, protection and correction they need as they serve the Lord in the local church.

If we have sin in our lives, the Lord instructs our church leaders to lovingly discipline us and restore us to walking in truth (1 Corinthians 5, Galatians 6:1, Matthew 18:17). Loving earthly fathers will discipline their children, in love, because they care for their children. God has chosen to use people as His rod to discipline us (2 Samuel 7:14), but the discipline is to reclaim us, not destroy us. Being disciplined shows God loves us. In fact, the Lord tells us in Hebrews 12:8, *If you are not disciplined (and everyone undergoes discipline), then you are illegitimate children and not true sons.*

Wherever you're committed in the body of Christ—in a small group (cell group), a local congregation or a house church—the Lord has called you to actively support and submit to the leadership He has placed there. If someone makes an accusation against a leader, tell that person to go directly

REFLECTION
What should happen if a leader has sin in his life (1 Timothy 5:19-20)? What should happen if we have sin in our lives?

to the leader. Do not pass on gossip or accusations. Do not allow gossip or slander to hinder the work of God in your midst. And remember, the Lord has placed godly authorities in our lives to help mold us into the character of Jesus Christ.

① He should be rebuked by 2-3 witnesses & publicly. (?)

② lovingly discipline us & restore us gently.

CHAPTER 3

The Blessing
of Authority

KEY MEMORY VERSE

For this reason I am sending to you Timothy,
my son whom I love, who is faithful in the Lord.
He will remind you of my way of life in
Christ Jesus, which agrees with what I teach
everywhere in every church.
1 Corinthians 4:17

Submission to authority brings protection

In this chapter, we will look at some of the blessings we receive when we submit to the authorities the Lord has placed in our lives. Some people grow up with a healthy understanding of honoring authority in their lives and realize it is there for their protection. Others rebel against authority because they have an improper understanding of it. The Lord desires to renew our minds by His Word so we can properly respect the delegated authorities He's placed in our lives.

First of all, submitting to authorities is a commandment of God. *Everyone must submit himself to the governing authorities, for there is no authority except that which God has established. The authorities that exist have been established by God. Consequently, he who rebels against the authority is rebelling against what God has instituted, and those who do so will bring judgment on themselves (Romans 13:1-2).* Here the scripture is talking about submitting to governing authorities, but it applies to all authorities in our lives. There is no authority except that which comes from God. In fact, God appoints the authorities that exist. In most cases, if we resist these authorities, we are resisting Him. We need to submit to the authorities that He's placed in our lives, because these authorities give us protection.

REFLECTION
Discuss the way God's authority acts like an umbrella.
How are the two forces in the universe controlling your life?

For example, if we disobey the speed limit, we could be killed or kill someone else. If a parent tells a child not to play with matches and he disobeys, there could be the loss of a home or the loss of life. It would not be the parents' fault or God's fault; the child simply disobeyed the authority that was placed in his life. He moved out from under the umbrella of God's protection.

Having an attitude of submission toward the authorities God has placed in our lives will protect us from many mistakes. It also is a protection against the influence of the devil. The nature of the devil is rebellion and deceit. Lucifer fell from heaven because he said, "I will be like the Most High." He refused to submit to God's authority.

In the universe there are two major forces—the one is submission to the authority of God, the other is rebellion. Whenever we allow an attitude of rebellion into our lives, we are beginning to be motivated by the enemy which leads us to sin against God.

28 ① Since He establishes the authorities over us we consequently are either faithful or rebellious to God & His authority. ② Constantly warring some w's some c's hopefully more w's

Submission to authority helps us learn principles of faith

In order to be people of faith who see miracles happen in our lives, we must understand the principles of authority. When we submit to the authorities in our lives, we learn the principles of faith. The faith of the centurion in Matthew 8:8-10 was tied into his understanding of authority. *The centurion replied, "Lord, I do not deserve to have you come under my roof. But just say the word, and my servant will be healed. For I myself am a man under authority, with soldiers under me. I tell this one, 'Go,' and he goes; and that one, 'Come,' and he comes. I say to my servant, 'Do this,' and he does it." When Jesus heard this, he was astonished and said to those following him, "I tell you the truth, I have not found anyone in Israel with such great faith."*

This centurion received a miracle from Jesus because he understood authority. As an officer, he could issue orders to his subordinates, and they would obey. He completely understood that Christ, who possesses all authority, could give a command, and His will would be done.

When Jesus says a sickness must go, it must leave. His life on this earth was filled with examples of healing people of various sicknesses and diseases. The scriptures teach us that we can expect miracles when we call for the elders of the church to pray for us if we are sick...*he should call the elders of the church to pray...and the prayer offered in faith will make the sick person well...(James 5:14-15).* The act of submitting to our spiritual leaders can release faith for healing in our lives!

REFLECTION
How can submitting to authority teach us about faith?
What does faith have to do with miracles?

Submission to authority trains us in character

Yet another blessing we receive from learning to submit to the authorities in our lives is that it trains us in character to be a loving authority to others.

The Lord uses authorities in our lives who speak the Word of God to us. His Word chips away from our lives anything that is not

Authority and Accountability

29

from Him. Just as a blacksmith takes a piece of iron, makes it hot so that it becomes pliable and chips the impurities away with his hammer, God's Word purifies. *"Is not my word like fire," declares the Lord...(Jeremiah 23:29).* It destroys all that is false in our lives and leaves only the genuine "metal." In the same way, our character is strengthened as we become conformed into the image of Christ.

God placed authorities in our lives to make us pliable. When we react to authority in anger and bitterness because we do not get our own way, it is probably a sign that there are still impurities the Lord is desiring to chip away from our lives. The Word of God is a purifying fire that changes us more into His likeness.

REFLECTION
How is God's Word shaping you? What is the Lord chipping away from your life? Which of the fruit(s) of the Spirit is it being replaced with?

If we haven't learned to submit to the authority in our lives in one setting, God will again bring someone into our new situation to whom we will have to learn to submit. He loves us that much. He is committed to seeing our lives motivated by the fruit of the Spirit: love, joy, peace, longsuffering, gentleness, goodness, faith, meekness and self-control (Galatians 5:22).

Submission to authority provides guidance

We will also find that submitting to the authority the Lord has placed in our lives often provides guidance for us to know His will. While growing up, my parents asked me to break off my relationship with certain ungodly friends. At the time, I did not appreciate what they were telling me. I felt controlled; but in retrospect, I am thankful to God for having submitted to their authority. I realize now, it saved me from having my life shipwrecked.

A contemporary Christian musician wanted to record an album; however, her parents asked her to wait. She found it difficult, but made a decision to submit to her parents. She later produced an album that has been a blessing to hundreds of thousands of people. God blessed this musician and gave her the right timing for the release of her album.

Joseph, in the Old Testament, submitted to the authority of the jailer, even though he was falsely imprisoned. The Lord later raised him up as prime minister for the whole nation.

① The word of God is a purifying fire that changes us more into His Likeness.

② Pride + selfishness

③ humility + patience.

30

Jesus himself submitted to His heavenly Father every day. Jesus says in John 5:30b...*for I seek not to please myself but him who sent me.* Jesus was committed to walking in submission to His heavenly Father's authority. Jesus did nothing of his own initiative, but only that which was initiated by His heavenly Father.

REFLECTION

To whose authority is Jesus submitted? How have you ever submitted to an authority in your life and discovered God's will for your life as a result?

What if the authority is wrong?

Many times people have asked me, "What should I do if the authority in my life is wrong?" As we mentioned before, we should obey God rather than man if the authority in our lives requires us to do something contrary to God's Word. But what if we believe the godly authority in our lives is making a mistake? Philippians 4:6 tells us to make an appeal. *Do not be anxious about anything, but in everything, by prayer and petition, with thanksgiving, present your requests to God.*

First of all, we need to appeal to God. We should pray, making known our requests and concerns, as we appeal to Him as our authority. In the same way, this sets a precedent for us to appeal to the delegated authorities in our lives. According to Webster's Dictionary, the word *appeal* means *an earnest entreaty or a plea.* The Lord wants us to appeal to the authorities He has placed in our lives with an attitude of submission.

Instead of having a submissive spirit and appealing to authority, Aaron and Miriam accused Moses regarding the leadership decisions that He was making. They did not fear God or respect God's prophet, and this allowed a spirit of rebellion to come into their lives. Moses, who had learned his lesson about authority in the desert while herding sheep, did not defend himself. Instead he went to God, and God defended him.

Daniel and his friends, in the Old Testament, appealed to the authority in their lives and asked only to eat certain foods (Daniel 1:8,12,13). The Lord honored their appealing to authority and blessed them with health, wisdom, literary skill and supernatural revelation.

Nehemiah appealed to the king to take a trip to Jerusalem (Nehemiah 1). His appeal to the authority in his life in an attitude of

① His Father ② Allowing myself to be submissive to Bob has allowed me to be a stronger steward over God's Finances in business. (4 Du I)

submission caused the king to grant his request. Nehemiah's attitude and obedience made it possible for the wall to be built around Jerusalem.

In conclusion, if any person in authority in our lives requires us to sin, we must obey God and not man (Acts 5:29). The early church leaders were told by the religious leaders of their day to stop proclaiming Jesus as Lord. They could not obey these orders; but, they still maintained a spirit and attitude of honoring the religious leaders. If the authorities in our lives are asking us to cheat, steal, lie, or sin in any way, we must obey the living God first! However, this is rarely the case. Usually God uses the authorities in our lives to help mold and structure our lives for good① I don't recall ⑴b ?

REFLECTION
Has there ever been a time when an authority wanted you to do something you knew was sin? What did you do?
What is often the result of appealing to authority?
What is the result of rebellion?

Maintain an attitude of love and submission

God's concern is that we have an attitude of love and submission to our God and to those He's placed in authority in our lives. This is often opposite of what we see today—people are more concerned about being right in their own eyes and insist on "doing their own thing."

Korah was a priest in the Old Testament who rose up in rebellion against Moses with 250 other leaders in Israel. Rather than appealing in love and submission to Moses' and Aaron's authority, they challenged their authority. *They came as a group to oppose Moses and Aaron and said to them, "You have gone too far! The whole community is holy, every one of them, and the Lord is with them. Why then do you set yourselves above the Lord's assembly?" (Numbers 16:3).*

Korah and the other leaders were rebellious. They thought they could choose for themselves who would lead God's people. But God made it certain; He was in charge. The next day, the ground opened up and swallowed all of them alive. God hates rebellion.

Abagail, in 1 Samuel 25, realized David and his army were coming to destroy her husband and their people. She went to David

② Reward + consideration of your position.

②b Its' own reward + entrenched opposition — it is folly.

and appealed to him, and he honored her and spared her family from death.

A friend of mine was required to sign a job-related document but realized that the technical wording would make him sign an untruth. He prayed and decided that he needed to obey God. Before he went to his supervisors to appeal to them, he asked the Lord for wisdom to fulfill his employer's intentions without compromising the truth. The Lord showed him a plan, but he was prepared to give up his job if required.

He told his supervisors he appreciated working at the company and explained why he could not sign the document. He admitted that it might inconvenience them or that he could lose his job; still, he needed to be faithful to God and not tell a lie. On his own time, he volunteered to make the change on the format of the document so it legally fulfilled their company's purpose at the same time. They accepted his idea, and the Lord gave him tremendous favor in that company. ① It is a act of humility + dependance upon Him + what He desires for us. It show postures our hearts correctly + puts the highest authority highest

Understanding delegated authority priority,

Sometime back, a missionary in a South American nation was teaching a Sunday School class on the subject of authority from Romans 13. A doctor stood up and said, "Do you mean that I must pay the taxes that my government requires?" At that time, this nation had a very ineffective tax collection system. Less than 25% of the entire population paid taxes. The government realized this so they raised the quota to four times more than what it should have been to cover the expenses for those who did not pay.

Convicted of this biblical principle, the doctor made a decision that day to pay his taxes, but he also prayed and asked the Lord for wisdom. The Lord gave the doctor an idea how to change the tax collection system. He shared his new idea with the city officials, and they adopted his suggestion. It worked so well that 80% of the people started paying their taxes. The state then adopted the plan which was later adopted by the whole nation. The entire nation was blessed through one man's obedience. Let us dare to obey the Word of God and see what He does through our obedience.

DAY 7

When we understand the principle of God's delegated authority, it changes the way we think. Paul, the apostle, clearly understood delegated authority. God had given Paul delegated authority, so Paul delegated some of the Lord's authority to Timothy and sent him to the Christians at Corinth. *For this reason I am sending to you Timothy, my son whom I love, who is faithful in the Lord. He will remind you of my way of life in Christ Jesus, which agrees with what I teach everywhere in every church (1 Corinthians 4:17).*

Years earlier, Paul, (then named Saul), was on the road to Damascus and blinded by a bright light. The Lord had instructed him to go into the city and have Ananias pray for him. Paul did not say, "But I want Peter, the apostle, to pray for me, or James." He was willing

REFLECTION
Name some people who have delegated authority over you in your family, church and workplace.

to receive prayer from the servant the Lord had chosen. Consequently, he was filled with the Holy Spirit and received his sight. Ananias probably was an "unknown" Christian in the church world at that time, but both Paul and Ananias understood the principle of God's delegated authority, and God honored them both.

①ₐ) My Father, my wife - submit yourselves one
   to another,
   b) Bob, MJ
   ©) Store, + customers.

The Blessing of Accountability

KEY MEMORY VERSE
Now I myself am confident concerning you,
my brethren, that you also are full of goodness,
filled with all knowledge,
able also to admonish one another.
Romans 15:14 NKJ

What is personal accountability?

The meaning of *accountability* is *to give an account to others for what God has called us to do.* We are first accountable to the Lord regarding how we live out our commitment to Christ. Our lives need to line up with the Word of God. Then we are accountable to fellow believers. These people are often the spiritual leaders God has placed in our lives. Hebrews 13:17 says these leaders are account-able to God concerning us because they...*keep watch over you as men who must give an account....*

Many times I've asked others to keep me accountable for a goal I believe the Lord has set for me. Several years ago I asked one of the men in a Bible study group in which I was involved to hold me accountable with my personal time in prayer and in meditating in God's Word each day. Every morning at 7:00 AM I received a phone call as my friend checked up on me. Accountability enabled me to be victorious. There is a tremendous release that happens in our lives when we are willing to ask others to hold us accountable for what the Lord has shown us for certain personal areas in our lives that need encouragement and support.

I want to emphasize that personal accountability is not having others tell us what to do. Personal accountability is finding out from God what He wants us to do and then asking others to hold us accountable to do those things. Spiritual abuse can occur when someone in a position of spiritual authority in our lives misuses that authority and attempts to control us. This is not biblical accountability! The purpose for someone in authority is to help build us up. If someone's seemingly "godly" accountability attempts to manipulate us rather than free us to do what God has called us to do, it is a misuse of power.

REFLECTION
Who "keeps watch over you"? Give an example of personal accountability from your own life.

Accountable to Jesus first

As we just mentioned, we are first accountable to the Lord as to how we live out our commitment to Him. Mark 6 shows how the twelve disciples were accountable to Jesus. He had trained them and now they were ready to be sent out on a task. In verse 7, Jesus sends them out two by two so they could comfort and support each other in their mission. *Calling the Twelve to him, he sent them out two by two and gave them authority over evil spirits.*

After they had ministered, verse 30 says that the disciples reported back to Jesus what they had experienced. This is an example of accountability in operation. *The apostles gathered around Jesus and reported to him all they had done and taught (Mark 6:7,30).*

Another time, when seventy-two disciples were sent out, they also came back and were accountable to Jesus. Luke 10:1,17 tells us, *After this the Lord appointed seventy-two others and sent them two by two ahead of him to every town and place where he was about to go. The seventy-two returned with joy and said, "Lord, even the demons submit to us in your name."*

REFLECTION

How were the disciples accountable to Jesus in Mark 6? How are you accountable to Jesus?

If the early disciples needed to be accountable to Jesus, the One who had sent them out, how much more we need to be accountable to our Lord Jesus Christ! We are accountable by living our lives in obedience to God's Word as we put our hope in His promises (Psalms 119:74) and hide it deep within our hearts (Psalms 119:11).

Accountable to others

We are often faced with serious spiritual battles that we must learn to overcome. Others can help us face those battles. Accountability consists of someone loving us enough to check up on us and seeing how we are doing in our personal lives so we can stay on track. Paul wrote to the Roman Christians to remind them of the truths they already knew. He wanted to encourage them to correct and hold each other accountable in a loving way. *Now I myself am confident concerning you, my brethren, that you also are full of goodness, filled with all knowledge, able also to admonish one another (Romans 15:14 NKJ).*

According to Webster's Dictionary, *admonish* means *to counsel against wrong practices, to caution or advise and to teach with correction.* We all need people in our lives to admonish us and hold us accountable. It doesn't just happen. We need to ask. *God resists the proud, but gives grace to the humble (1 Peter 5:5b).* It takes humility to ask others to hold us accountable for the way we live our Christian lives, but God gives grace to those who are humble and willing to open their lives to others.

One time, after spending a few days praying with a group of Christian leaders, I asked one of the fellow leaders to hold me accountable for the way I conducted myself as a Christian leader. He consented and asked me to do the same for him. There is tremendous freedom and protection in being accountable to someone else. The devil dwells in darkness and will try to isolate us from other believers. Jesus desires for us to walk in the light of openness and accountability.

REFLECTION
What does admonish *mean? Have you ever humbled yourself to ask another person to hold you accountable? What happened?*

Accountability helps us stand under temptation

Many times a Christian will begin to grow in his Christian life and then fall back into a mediocre Christian experience. Other times believers are overtaken by temptation and fall into sin. Accountability to another person helps us to stay on fire for God and stand up under temptation...*God is faithful; he will not let you be tempted beyond what you can bear. But when you are tempted, he will also provide a way out so that you can stand up under it (1 Corinthians 10:13).*

We should not be afraid to be honest about our struggles and shortfalls. One of the benefits of accountability is that often we find that we are not the only one who struggles in a particular area. Knowing we are not alone with our problems helps us to be more transparent to admit our weaknesses so we can be healed. *Therefore confess your sins to each other and pray for each other so that you may be healed (James 5:16).*

Who are the people the Lord has placed in your life? Ask them to hold you accountable to do what the Lord has called you to do. Perhaps you need accountability in handling your finances properly. Or perhaps you need to be accountable for how you relate to your spouse.

If you desire to lose weight, you'll find a tremendous blessing in being accountable to someone for your eating habits and daily exercise. I once heard a man say that he had lost over 20,000 pounds in his lifetime. He would lose a few pounds and then gain the weight back, lose it again, then gain it back again. The cycle went on and on. Although he was exaggerating and joking about his physical condition, the truth is, he desperately needed to be accountable to someone in his life. Accountability is freeing! It encourages us to move on to maturity and victory in our lives.

REFLECTION
How has God used other people to help you stand up under temptation? Have you ever helped someone else be accountable to God? What does Hebrews 3:13 tell us to do daily?

Accountability keeps us from becoming lazy in our relationship with the Lord and provides a "way out" for us when temptation hits. The Bible tells us to encourage one another daily, so we do not become hardened by sin's deceitfulness (Hebrews 3:13).

Accountability helps us with "blind spots"

DAY 5

Many drivers experience what we call a "blind spot" while passing, turning or backing up their vehicle. In this potentially dangerous blind spot, it is impossible to see oncoming traffic.

In the same way, many of us have blind spots in our lives that we often miss but others can see. There are many people in our lives that can help us with the blind spots. These people can hold us accountable as to how we are living our lives. At work, we may be accountable to a foreman. In the home, husbands and wives are accountable to one another. Children are accountable to their parents. We are accountable to the leaders in our church. The scriptures tell us in Proverbs 11:14...*in the multitude of counselors there is safety (NKJ)*. A friend of mine once said, "Learn to listen to your critics. They may tell you things that your friends may never tell you." This is good advice.

Something to remember when we hold others accountable is that we should not judge their attitudes. Instead, we help them see certain actions in their lives that may be displeasing to the Lord. We should speak it in a way that will encourage them. We are accountable for the words we speak. *But I tell you that men will have to give account on the day of judgment for every careless word they have spoken. For by your words you will be acquitted, and by your words you will be condemned (Matthew 12:36-37).*

At one point in my Christian life, I was convicted by the Lord to develop a more intimate relationship with Him. I shared honestly about this need in my life with one of the men in my small group. There were certain things that I knew I needed to do to pursue my relationship with Jesus, and this Christian friend "checked up on me" or held me accountable by encouraging me to do them.

Matthew 18 describes a slightly different case scenario of accountability in the church. When a professing Christian brother or sister sins against us privately, what should we do to hold them accountable to that sin? This scripture says we should not go to someone else about the problem. We must love the offender enough to go directly to him. If he has sin in his life and does not receive you, the Bible says we should then take one or two Christian friends along and talk to him again (Matthew 18:15-17). The goal is to see him restored and healed.

REFLECTION
What is a "blind spot"? Has anyone ever helped you with one? What are the accountability steps listed in Matthew 18 to handle a problem between you and another Christian?

The goal of accountability is always to reach out in love and humility to an individual so that he receives a reaffirmation of God's love in his life and is restored to Christlikeness.

Accountability in a small group

DAY 6

God did not create us to live without fellowshipping with other believers. When it comes to the everyday experience of living for Jesus, we need people in our lives with whom we are in close relationship to encourage us.

And let us consider how we may spur one another on toward love and good deeds. Let us not give up meeting together, as some are in the habit of doing, but let us encourage one another—and all the more as you see the Day approaching (Hebrews 10:24-25).

If one falls down, his friend can help him up. But pity the man who falls and has no one to help him up! (Ecclesiastes 4:10).

Fellow believers can help to keep us accountable to those things the Lord is saying to us. A small group of believers in a Sunday School class, a cell group, a youth group or in a house church is a

Biblical Foundations

great place to express the desire for accountability. We cannot be accountable to everyone in a large setting, but in a small group of people we can more easily share our struggles and receive the help we need to overcome a problem or temptation.

In a small group, we can be trained, equipped and encouraged in the things of God. No one should try to live his or her Christian life without the support of others. We can save ourselves many heartaches by learning the principle of accountability and applying it to our lives within a small group.

REFLECTION

According to Hebrews 10:25, why is it important to fellowship with other believers?

Why is it easier to be accountable to others in a small group?

Our ultimate authority is Jesus

Our ultimate authority and accountability must come from Jesus, not from other people. Jesus gives us His authority to live victorious lives. *I have given you authority to trample on snakes and scorpions and to overcome all the power of the enemy; nothing will harm you (Luke 10:19).*

Jesus is the One from whom we receive authority. Even though God uses delegated authorities in our lives and requires us to have an attitude of submission to them, God is the one who gives us ultimate authority. We even have authority over the demons in Jesus' name because of the authority of Jesus Christ. When we receive that authority by knowing Him and living in an intimate relationship with Jesus, His Word gives us authority.

When Jesus spoke, people listened. As we draw close to Jesus, we also will speak with the authority of Jesus Christ. *When Jesus had finished saying these things, the crowds were amazed at his teaching, because he taught as one who had authority, and not as their teachers of the law (Matthew 7:28-29).*

God is restoring the fear of the Lord in our generation. He has called us to submit to the authorities He's placed in our lives. As we submit to these authorities, the Lord teaches us the principles of faith. The Lord gives authority to His delegated authorities to mold, shape, and form us into the image of Christ. These authorities are found in governments, places of work, in our families, in our communities, and in our church.

The Lord has called us to have an attitude of submission to the authorities He's placed in our lives, realizing that ultimate authority is His. We should never obey any authority that is causing us to sin (Acts 5:29). We must obey God rather than man. If we believe the authorities in our lives are causing us to sin, we need to pray and appeal to them.

Who are the authorities the Lord has placed in your life? Who is holding you accountable? A proper understanding of authority and accountability brings tremendous security and freedom to us. Knowing that the Lord loves us enough to place authorities in our lives to protect us and to mold us is wonderful! To know that the people the Lord has placed in our lives love us enough to hold us accountable with our actions is a tremendous blessing. We do not have to live our Christian lives alone! God bless you as you experience the loving authority of Jesus Christ and the blessing of accountability.

REFLECTION
The very authority of God is given to His people on the earth! Describe this power (Luke 10:19). What does a proper understanding of authority and accountability bring into our lives?

Understanding the Fear of the Lord and Authority

1. The fear of the Lord causes us to obey

a. The fear of the Lord causes people to place their faith in the Lord for salvation (Jonah 1:16).

b. God judges sin because He is a holy God so we should want to obey.

2. The fear of the Lord causes us to reverence God

a. A deep reverence and love for God helps us gain wisdom. Proverbs 9:10

b. We should possess a healthy fear that trembles at God's Word (Isaiah 66:2).

c. A fear of the Lord involves a fear of sinning against Him and facing the consequences.

d. We should not be afraid (1 John 4:18) but fear the consequences of the discipline that follows disobedience.

3. The fear of the Lord causes us to turn away from evil

a. We will not want to sin if we have the fear of the Lord. Proverbs 8:13

b. We will hate evil knowing that evil displeases the Lord and destroys us (1 Corinthians 6:9-11).

c. Our fear of the Lord is not a destructive fear but one that leads us to God's presence (Revelation 1:17).

4. Why authorities are placed in our lives

a. Authorities are in our lives to mold us, adjust us and structure our lives.

b. If we resist authorities, we are resisting God. Romans 13:1-4

c. Authority brings security (Romans 13:3). Without authority, there is chaos (Judges 21:25).

d. God delegates authority to men and women. Anyone who has authority needs to be under authority.

5. What does it mean to submit to authority?

a. We should be obedient to authorities in our lives (Titus 3:1).

b. Submission may seem foolish (1 Corinthians 1:27) but when we resist authority, we are resisting God (unless the authority is asking you to do something that violates God's Word and causes you to sin).

6. Obedience is better than "sacrifice"

a. God requires obedience to His Word. Saul rebelled and disobeyed God's clear instructions and placed his own perception of what was right above what God said. God equated his rebellion with witchcraft (1 Samuel 15:22-23).

b. Obeying from the heart is better than sacrifice (outward forms of service for the Lord).

7. Delegated authority molds us

a. We do not submit to authorities because they are perfect, but because God has placed them there.

b. Delegated authorities have been appointed by the Lord (Luke 17:7-10) and it is our responsibility to obey.

Delegated Authority in Government, Workplace, Family and Church

1. **Honoring authority in government**
    a. We need restraints to protect us (Romans 13:1-2).
    b. We keep a clear conscience by obeying governing authorities (Romans 13:5-7).
    c. We should obey even ungodly authorities (Acts 23:3). Honor their position, not their conduct.

2. **Honoring authority in the workplace**
    a. Our jobs are like service to the Lord (Colossians 3:22-24).
    b. Our real employer is Jesus Christ, and our jobs are like serving Him as we work.

3. **How God uses employers in our lives**
    a. Submitting to a boss' authority teaches us discipline.
        1 Timothy 6:1-2; 1 Peter 2:18-21
    b. Jesus and Moses submitted to their employer's authority before the Lord used them effectively.
        Mark 6:3; Exodus 3

4. **Honoring authority in the family**
    a. God commands children to obey their parents (Ephesians 6:1-4) and promises a long life if they do.
    b. Parents should honor their children too (Colossians 3:21) by bringing them up in the instruction of the Lord without discouraging them.
    c. Should parents be obeyed if they ask their children to do something against God's Word? (Acts 5:29)

5. Submit to each other in the home
   a. Mutual submission is a biblical principle applied to Christian families (Ephesians 5:21-23).
   b. The husband heads the family team (Ephesians 6:25).

6. Honoring authority in the church
   a. Spiritual leaders watch out for us (Hebrews 13:17).
   b. We must honor these leaders (1 Thessalonians 5:12-13).
   c. Spiritual authority and servanthood go hand-in-hand. Matthew 20:25-28

7. Sin in a spiritual leader's life
   a. We cannot blindly submit to a leader who falls into sin. We should confront him (1 Timothy 5:19-20).
   b. Those over him in authority are responsible to discipline him.
   c. If there is sin in our lives, church leaders should lovingly discipline us (1 Corinthians 5, Galatians 6:1, Matthew 18:17) and restore us to walking in truth.
   d. Being disciplined by God shows He loves us. Hebrews 12:8

The Blessing of Authority

1. Submission to authority brings protection

a. Submitting to authorities is a commandment of God. Romans 13:1-2

b. No authority exists except that which comes from God. They are in place for our protection. Submitting to them protects us from mistakes and the influence of the devil.

c. Two major forces in this world: submission to authority and rebellion.

2. Submission to authority helps us learn principles of faith

a. The faith of the centurion was tied into his understanding of authority (Matthew 8:8-10).

b. He understood that Christ, who possesses all authority, could give a command and His will would be done.

c. The act of submitting to leaders can release healing in our lives (James 5:14-15).

3. Submission to authority trains us in character

a. The Lord uses authorities in our lives who speak the Word of God to us. His Word is like a hot fire that melts away from our lives anything that is not from Him (Jeremiah 23:29).

b. God placed authorities in our lives to make us pliable. He wants to see us motivated by the fruit of the Spirit. Galatians 5:22

4. Submission to authority provides guidance

a. Joseph submitted to the authority of the jailor even though he was falsely imprisoned. The Lord later raised him up as prime minister.

b. Jesus submitted to His Father every day (John 5:30) to provide guidance to know His will.

5. What if the authority is wrong?

a. If we believe an authority in our lives is making a mistake, we make an appeal to God (Philippians 4:6).

b. This sets the precedent for appealing to the authorities God has placed in our lives.

Ex: Aaron and Miriam accused Moses rather than appealing to his authority, and a spirit of rebellion came into their lives.

Ex: Daniel humbly appealed to authorities by asking to eat certain foods, and the Lord honored his appeal. Daniel 1:8,12,13

c. If a person in authority requires us to sin, we must obey God and not man (Acts 5:29).

6. Maintain an attitude of love and submission

a. Rather than appealing in love and submission to his authority, Korah and some other leaders rose in rebellion against Moses (Numbers 16:3). The ground opened up and swallowed them.

b. We must maintain an attitude of love and submission to our leaders.

7. Understanding delegated authority

a. Understanding delegated authority changes the way we think.

Ex: A man in a developing country was not paying taxes, because of the ineffective system. He was convicted to obey his governmental authorities and thought of a way to change the system. The government adopted his idea.

b. Paul sent Timothy to the Corinth church with his delegated authority (1 Corinthians 4:17).

The Blessing of Accountability

1. **What is personal accountability?**
   a. Accountability is giving an account to others for what God has called us to do.
   b. Spiritual abuse happens if someone in a position of authority attempts to control us by "accountability." Manipulation is a misuse of power.

2. **Accountable to Jesus first**
   a. We are first accountable to Jesus as to how we live out our commitment to Him.
   b. Jesus sent His disciples out and they later reported back to Him (Mark 6:7,30; Luke 10:1,17).

3. **Accountable to others**
   a. Accountability is someone loving us enough to check up on us and helping us stay on track (Romans 15:14). The NKJ says we should *admonish* each other.
   b. *Admonish* means *to advise and teach with correction.*

4. **Accountability helps us stand under temptation**
   a. Accountability is not being afraid to admit our weaknesses. We can have our accountability partner pray with us about it for healing (James 5:16).
   b. Accountability keeps us from getting lazy in our relationship with the Lord and provides a "way out" when temptation hits (1 Corinthians 10:13).

5. Accountability helps us with "blind spots"

a. Others in our lives can help us with blind spots: Husbands, wives, children, employers, church leaders (Proverbs 11:14).

b. When we hold others accountable, we should not judge their attitudes but encourage them and help them see certain actions that displease the Lord. We are accountable for the words we speak (Matthew 12:36-37).

c. Steps of accountability in the church: Matthew 18:15-17. The goal is to restore to Christlikeness.

6. Accountability in a small group

a. Be accountable to fellow believers in a small group setting. Hebrews 10:24-25, Ecclesiastes 4:10

b. No one should attempt to live his Christian life alone, without the encouragement of other believers.

7. Our ultimate authority is Jesus

a. Although God uses delegated authority in our lives and requires us to submit to them, God is the ultimate authority, not other people.

b. Jesus gives us authority to live supernatural, victorious lives. Luke 10:19

c. An understanding of authority and accountability brings freedom in our lives.

d. Who are the authorities the Lord placed in your life? Who is holding you accountable?

Chapter 1
Understanding the Fear of the Lord and Authority
Journaling space for reflection questions

DAY 1 *In the story of Jonah, how did the sailor's fear of their heathen gods differ from the fear of the Lord they experienced in Jonah 1:16?*

DAY 2 *If God does not want us to be afraid of Him, what kind of "fear" are we talking about?*

DAY 3 *What do we hate when we have a healthy fear of the Lord, according to Proverbs 8:13? What does the fear of the Lord lead us to?*

Who are the governing authorities in your life? List ways each one is used by the Lord to mold, adjust and structure your life.

What does authority mean? How is resisting authority in your life actually resisting God?

What did Saul do that displeased God so much? Explain the phrase "obedience is better than sacrifice."

Put yourself in the place of the servant in this story. What would your attitude be?

Chapter 2
Delegated Authority in Government, Workplace, Family and Church
Journaling space for reflection questions

Why should we be careful who we call a "whitewashed wall"?
Why should we honor governmental authorities?

How are we really working for "employer" Jesus Christ on our jobs? What should our attitude be toward our employers?

How should we act if we are disciplined on the job by a believing boss for doing something wrong?
How is Jesus our example in the matter of submission?

DAY 4

What is the promise for those who honor their parents (Ephesians 6:1-4)? According to Acts 5:29, what should we do if an authority in our lives asks us to do something that is sinful?

DAY 5

How do husbands and wives submit to each other? Who should take leadership for the husband-wife team?

DAY 6

How do we honor spiritual authorities in our lives? What are the things our spiritual authorities do for us?

DAY 7

What should happen if a leader has sin in his life (1 Timothy 5:19-20)? What should happen if we have sin in our lives?

Chapter 3
The Blessing of Authority
Journaling space for reflection questions

DAY 1
Discuss the way God's authority acts like an umbrella.
How are the two forces in the universe controlling your life?

DAY 2
How can submitting to authority teach us about faith?
What does faith have to do with miracles?

DAY 3
How is God's Word shaping you? What is the Lord chipping away
from your life? Which of the fruit(s) of the Spirit is it being replaced
with?

DAY 4 To whose authority is Jesus submitted? How have you ever submitted to an authority in your life and discovered God's will for your life as a result?

DAY 5 Has there ever been a time when an authority wanted you to do something you knew was sin? What did you do? What is often the result of appealing to authority? What is the result of rebellion?

DAY 6 Why does God want you to appeal to Him when you have a problem submitting to an authority?

DAY 7 Name some people who have delegated authority over you in your family, church and workplace.

Chapter 4
The Blessing of Accountability
Journaling space for reflection questions

DAY 1

Who "keeps watch over you"? Give an example of personal accountability from your own life. primary - Bob Preston
backups - Rick+ Julie   back ups - Johnny Cawthen.

Since the business God gave me as a ministry
+ my spiritual walk are webbed together, I have
the fortunate pleasure of having my brother Bob
Preston to help guide me + mentor me when my sight
is short, my perspective narrowed, my mind closed + my
behavior + attitude become out of skew.

DAY 2

How were the disciples accountable to Jesus in Mark 6?
How are you accountable to Jesus?

① After He sent them out + then their
return they had to give report of
what they had done + the fruits of their
learning.

② By living our lives in obedience to
His Word. We rest our faith + hope in
His promises. And continually fellowshipping
with Him as He resides deep in our hearts.

DAY 3

What does admonish mean? Have you ever humbled yourself to ask another person to hold you accountable?
What happened?

① Counsel against wrong practices, caution + advise,
+ to teach with correction.
② Yes. He still does + it's still hard +
humbling.

How has God used other people to help you stand up under temptation? Have you ever helped someone else be accountable to God? What does Hebrews 3:13 tell us to do daily?

① They pray for + encourage me - my third ~~second~~ biggest cheer leader after ~~Christ thru~~ Christ + my wife. ② Yes ③ encourage one another.

What is a "blind spot"? Has anyone ever helped you with one? What are the accountability steps listed in Matthew 18 to handle a problem between you and another Christian?

① A place in a persons area of sight that can not be seen easily or at all. ② Yes ③ Go to them privately, then w/ two or three, then with the church.

According to Hebrews 10:24-25, why is it important to fellowship with other believers? Why is it easier to be accountable to others in a small group? ① We need people in our lives whom are close to us in relationship to encourage us + spur us on toward Christ → our goal.

② In a small setting we can more easily share our struggles + ~~temptations~~ + receive the help we need to overcome them.

The very authority of God is given to His people on the earth! Describe this power (Luke 10:19). What does a proper understanding of authority and accountability bring into our lives?

① We, because of our relationship w/ Christ can petition Him in prayer, He being our advocate, + ultimate authority has the ability to change the ~~er~~ very circumstance we're in — even over the authority whom He placed over you + me. ② Liberty, freedom, security

Authority and Accountability

Daily Devotional Extra Days

If you are using this book as a daily devotional, you will notice there are 28 days in this study. Depending on the month, you may need the three extra days' studies given here.

God's Delegated Authority

Review the first four days of Chapter Three and find six blessings we receive when we submit to God's delegated authority. List various scriptures that have special meaning to you that you have learned. Examine your own life to see if you are submitting to the authorities over you.

Are You Under God's Umbrella?

List the four areas of God's delegated authority mentioned in this book. Give scriptures for each of these four areas. Trace the authority of God down to you. Do you know who is over you? Are you under the umbrella of God's protective authority?

Understanding Authority and Accountability

List various verses that helped you understand accountability. What verses or story in these lessons helped you understand authority and accountability and your need to submit to it? Explain.